CHURCH OF SHADOW AND LIGHT

Church

of

Shadow

and

Light

POEMS

HEIDI BARR

WAYFARER BOOKS
ABIQUIU, NEW MEXICO

WWW.WAYFARERBOOKS.ORG

Published in 2025 by Wayfarer Books
Cover Design and Interior Design by Connor Wolfe
Cover Image © Bernd Dittrich
TRADE PAPERBACK 9781965320341

10 9 8 7 6 5 4 3 2 1

Look for our titles in paperback, ebook, and audiobook wherever books are sold.
Wholesale offerings for retailers available through Ingram.

Wayfarer Books is committed to ecological stewardship.
We greatly value the natural environment and invest in conservation.

PO Box 1109, Abiquiu, New Mexico
wayfarer@homeboundpublications.com
WAYFARERBOOKS.ORG

For the peacemakers

CONTENTS

Shadow

Light

Church

"Once there was a man who was afraid of his shadow.

Then he met it.

Now he glows in the dark."

—BEN LOORY

Stories for Nighttime and Some for the Day

COEXISTING

Do you ever wonder about what truth and beauty really look like? Or how shadow and light are both necessary to create that truth and beauty? I think about that a lot—about how truth and beauty and shadow and light find ways to carry us through hard things; about all the people in the world who feel lost in forests of hopelessness; about how far away peace often feels.

I think about what Rumi wrote so long ago:
"When I go toward you | it is with my whole life."

What's worth going toward with a whole life? That's one of those questions that doesn't have "one right answer." Kind of like there's no one right answer to "who or what is God?"

So I wonder about the questions that don't have one right answer, and how those questions matter. I also wonder about the questions that don't have any answers at all.

Consider what happens when you ask a forest what's important and it doesn't respond. What if you took the silence as an invitation to find your own truth on a forgotten path, one that's uncovered only by walking the edges of unanswerable questions? Sometimes it's the path leading deep into the shadows that allows a way forward to rise up in a language only light can translate.

It's not easy to accept the invitation to walk the paths that require living the questions. Yet even though there is nothing but mystery inside such an invitation, there is also comfort, or maybe something more like reassurance, in allowing all things to be possible.

I think about the church of shadow and light, about how we know our holy places by how accepting they are of our whole personhood, by what we'll endure to be there to pray, by the simple knowledge that something shifts each time we show up. I think about truth and beauty and how they are found inside shadow and light, and the peace that shows up when we allow both to exist.

Shadow

shad·ow/ˈSHadō/*noun*

a dark area or shape produced by a body
coming between rays of light and a surface.

BEAUTY, ANYWAY,
DURING A WINTER THAT WASN'T

Find faith
in fleeting frost
in daybreak shadows
in too warm mornings
that hold you anyway
as you walk through
woods that sparkle
despite everything.

SACRED STRETCH

Go to the darkening places
where emotion stands tall
making even home ground feel shaky
and ask a silhouette to dance.
Invite someone you trust
to be there with you
in acknowledgment of what is—
even hard places soften
when allowed to move true.

STORIES IN THE WATER

I see stories in puddles dotting lake ice
trying to hold on—lake ice not quite ready
to acquiesce to warmth's transition.
Or maybe it's just me that's not ready,
during a winter that never really was, a winter
of unwanted flame and feelings of being cast aside, a winter
that held too much of some things and not enough of others.
Those stories dotting the lake
tell tales of letting go, of reflection,
of seeing beauty existing alongside lament.
Those stories contain truth, the kind of truth
you have to allow in, be patient enough to uncover.
I see stories in puddles dotting the lake ice—
stories that reach across the unwanted
through ripples of winter's warmth
to offer love through loss.

WAITING FOR SUNRISE

How do you capture fog
racing across newly open water
on a morning when chill laces the air
and bird song fills the stillness?
You can't, not really—
because wild beauty isn't containable
by photograph or word or even memory.
But it can be existed within,
every moment of your attention
becoming part of who you are,
claiming you as part of what's true.

PROOF OF LIFE IN A JANUARY WOOD

Grass and sticks woven
together in anticipation, a tiny home
perched in a dormant sapling.

Tracks big and small
claws and toe and tail marks
evidence of wild crossroads.

Moss, persistently green
even while the world is frozen,
dormant, but always ready for thaw.

A drumming in the trees
woodpecker's reminder that shadow seasons
offer ample opportunity to excavate hidden treasures.

ON EXISTING

Give shape to your world.
Make it a place to be free.
Mold life by moment.

WHEN LANGUAGE HAS SOMETHING ELSE TO SAY TO YOU

In the aftermath of loss

it's hard to find words, some days.
What is there to say that would make things better?

What happened, happened.
No words can undo that, and no words can fix it.

This could be reason for despair
(and it's fair to rage and grieve) or

this could be reason to look beyond words
deeply into unexplored ways of interacting with what isn't wanted.

In the aftermath of loss

it's hard to find words—so what is there to find outside
the confines of language spoken or signed?

Language felt, like a cold wind you don't welcome,
but feel fully anyway, contrast waking you up in new ways.

Language tasted, like a kumquat bursting on your tongue,
startling sour followed by a sweetness only reached by piercing skin.

Language seen, like a ray of light streaming in from so far away
it's barely reached you. But it has reached you, even now,

in the aftermath of loss.

HIRAETH

*Welsh; loosely translated to mean to be homesick
for a place you have never been*

I'm listening to a bittersweet symphony
songs from the 90s filling the evening
as I look at a sunset photograph
of a far off land, one unknown to me—
unfamiliar trees reaching
toward fading rainbows of light,
and I want to be walking that road
gazing at those distant hills—
it's another version of bittersweet,
the sort that rises from being fully
content where you are, while longing
to be a place you've never been,
remembering eras gone by,
magic of the mystical unknown
and energy of another time
undercurrents of the song.

SAVING ROOM FOR POSSIBILITIES

Leaving room
for possibility
means learning
to be okay
existing in liminality–
leaning deeply
into the mystery
of what could be next.

A BOWL OF CHERRIES

I buy myself the bag of expensive cherries
[on impulse or maybe on instinct, sometimes it's hard to tell which]
the day before a third interview for a job that could pay all the bills—
bills that continue demanding attention despite inadequate income,
despite a job market that isn't life-giving enough for a human worker,
despite all the unpaid labor that continues to be necessary—
a job that would be good to have, but a job that will demand keeping
a schedule not mine, a job providing tasks to fill empty space
created by other tasks that vanished months ago, empty space
that seemed so very bleak for a while, but empty space
full of opportunities to practice moving more slowly,
with reason to consider what it is I really do want—
anyway, I bought the expensive cherries
and washed them in cold water
and then I dropped them into a wooden bowl;
a small act of rebellion, a nod toward confidence,
or perhaps just so I can have an edible talisman,
a way to ingest possibility, a way to claim agency
in a world that feels like too much,
a way of allowing truth and beauty
to carry a beacon through shadows.

HARD, BUT NOT IMPOSSIBLE

Forgive who you were
when you tried to beat yourself
in a fight you knew you couldn't win.

Notice the still part
deep within, the part of you
that knows how to talk to clouds.

Look all the way up.
Remember who you are
when you're in the conversation, not the fight.

WHEN BEAUTY LOOKS DIFFERENT THAN YOU THINK IT SHOULD

One evening, three months after the world turns upside down
I'm watching dusk fall over the lake,
tawny reflections in conversation
with red winged birds,
thinking of all the ways falling
brings beauty into the story—
dusk falling over still water
rain falling into pools of silver shimmer
willow branches falling in a living curtain of green—
and I wonder how our own falling
brings beauty with it.
When the rug is swept from under your feet,
you can close your eyes and wish it different
or you can widen your gaze to take in the new view.
Because what if that view includes
daytime stars fading
dragonflies drifting
dawn rising,
transforming what's fallen
into a mosaic capable of lifting
shadows toward light?

A PRACTICE OF DISCERNMENT

First, avoid scheduling your epiphanies,
and leave ample room for slowly questioning
where beauty lives inside tarnished pots
or how snails cultivate time.
Next, set aside everything you think you know
about what you're trying to figure out
and consider what possibilities exist
when everything is mystery.
Let that not knowing lead directly
toward the heart of the inquiry, along
with any answers found by accepting
there is no one right way to find your way—
there is just the practice of listening to what
wants to speak through you as discovery
learns where you rest your head at night.
You may find you've been on the path all along,
even if very little becomes clear as you find
a new appreciation for the soft fog of ambiguity.

FLEXIBILITY

Let that ambiguity
wrap you up like a blanket,
but not the kind that makes you stay still—
more like the kind you wear as soft armor
with enough give to take you anywhere—
even straight into the howling wind.

LIGHT IN THE DARK SEASON

What happens when you draw
your attention to light—especially
on dark or shadowy days?
Light from a low flame dancing
flickers and follows no set path.
Light from twinkly holiday bulbs
reflects softly in panes of glass.
Light from sun when the day is gray
seems flat yet somehow still illuminates time.
Light in stars feels cold and distant
until you remember light streaming
in from so far away has been persistently
unwavering in its quest to find you.

BY THE RIVER

Ada Limón, in a poem called *Wonder Woman,*
talks about being by the river, indestructible,
an idea that finds me on a day I feel anything but–
indestructible? Ha. These days even a slight breeze
threatens to knock what little stability lingers
straight to the late winter ground, ground that feels
rockier than before, ground that undulates
with uncertainty and too much scrolling.
Wonder Woman is a myth that feels far from these shores,
these shores that hold breaking and grief and destruction
yet there's a woman, still, by the river, indestructible
water running parallel to that rocky ground
and in that river there's a reflection of a woman
shaky but more stable than she thinks.

CREATURELINESS

Were you the mink
rarely seen, almost an apparition
making a home by the lake,
unannounced and glad of it.

You would stalk solitude
like the heron stalks fish:
still and silent until moving
becomes essential for survival.

You would go about your days
content with what is,
centered in the truth
that just living is enough.

So find your creatureliness
in how your feet touch the ground,
carrying you forward, sometimes, and
sometimes not, like on days time stands still

or seems to move backward. Find it
in how your face turns toward sun
shining warmth on a cold day, or how
mist rising from the lake coats your skin

with a cloak of contrast. Find it
in the way a cool drink of water
revives your spirit and refreshes your senses.
Find it in the way your nose seeks scent,

luring you toward nourishment or how your tongue
helps you turn food into life's energy. Find it
in how you prowl the night when you can't sleep
and how you cradle your young in a nest of your own making.

Find your creatureliness deep within
where it has always been and will always be.
Go about your days content with what is,
centered in the truth that just living is enough.

HOW TO ALWAYS BE EMPLOYED
EVEN IF IT DOESN'T PAY WELL

Go to where water falls
in ribbons onto sculptures of ice.
Stand quietly enough to melt
into the rhythm of the rocks.
Practice being attentive
to sound echoing and scent rising
always feeling your way toward
how wonder fills the empty space
to soften the rough edge of uncertainty.

A BLESSING FOR EXISTING IN A BURNING WORLD

Maybe it all vanished
so abruptly it felt like there was nothing
but shock to take with you
on the unwanted journey ahead.

Maybe what came next has felt
full of firmly closed doors
or doors that open just enough
to allow a glimpse of what could have been.

Maybe those doors
are connected by paths
lined with thorns created
by the pairing of fear and desire.

Maybe (likely)
you're tired and ready
for something, anything
to be different.

At any rate, despite
what has or hasn't happened
in the weeks between before
and now—

May the journey ahead
become yours, even if the origin wasn't.

May the journey ahead be full of doors
that open toward knowing your worth.

May the journey ahead connect you to the joy
created by existing in community.

May the journey ahead find you bearing witness
to the beauty of the light that's still present
even in a burning world.

DAYDREAMS AND SPARKS

Remember what you dream in daylight.

Feel a way forward in the dark.

See beauty in that which remains.

Let it be a spark worth following.

EARTHBOUND STARS

Send your prayers
to the branches
and bear witness.

Let love wrap them
with the brilliance of stars,
each one eventually falling

rushing toward earth
to nourish any shadowy places
in need of just a bit more brightness.

WRITE WHAT YOU WISH YOU DIDN'T KNOW

I want to say I quit my job
to be a poet

but that's not what happened.
Instead life got turned upside down

by a layoff—a quitting of work, yes,
but not on the timeline of my choosing.

I want to say the need for money
vanished along with the regular paycheck

but that's not what happened either.
Instead the need for work continued,

demanding time and energy and applications
asking for a role that would demand time and energy,

energy I'd rather spend noticing glimmers
of light frolicking across a frosty morning.

So, I want to say I quit my job
to be a poet

but that's not what happened.
Instead what happened was words

found me anyway, arranging themselves
like they belonged together on the page

a flow of image and ideas that rose up, and rise up still,
not due to devoting life to the craft

but rather by allowing the craft to mold life,
moment by moment, attention my devotion

naming the ache,
but also celebrating the season

amidst the to-dos and the missing pieces,
around the need to work and maybe even because of it–

After all, reality is where poems take root, meandering through
ordinary mystical, shadowy things, and poets, well,

(no matter our employment status)
we notice, and tell about it.

Light

/līt/ *noun*

the natural agent that stimulates sight
and makes things visible.

WHAT I SEE WHEN I DREAM OF LIGHT

Three trees
in a wood full of stars
each one dancing in time
to what roots love to earth.

INSTRUCTIONS FOR LIVING

No one can tell another
how to live—so be wary
of anybody selling that particular
brand of promise. There is no way
you'll get your money's worth.
Rather, go get some seeds,
or a pair of snowshoes, or adopt
a creaturely companion to keep you
company on the trail—anything
that gets you outside, interacting
with wild things like soil and snow
and your own breath meeting air
as you move through the woods—
anything that reminds you you're alive
and it's time to pay attention
to the path you're on.

BIOLUMINESCENCE

There they go, swimming in the sky
all sharp tongues and soft teeth, skin
of feathers and buoyant bones, unexpected
details forming a new picture in your mind's eye—
a different sort of creature full of energy showing up
in ways that are outside the small box of normality,
coaxing you to see with new eyes, eyes that smell
and taste and feel and ride on wings of lightning
tracing the shadows of a bright, fluid night.

FINDING THE WORLD
IN A SINGLE LEAF

Water droplets
on fallen foliage,
tiny universes, each one
a glimpse of what happens
when the gardener of time
weeps in celebration
of the season.

HOW TO SEE NORTHERN LIGHTS

First, if possible, ensure home
is a place where such viewing happens,
at least sometimes, or visit often where it does.
Second, pay attention to the horizon at night
while practicing patience—it could take awhile.
Years, in fact, but don't let the elusiveness
of aurora borealis stop you from venturing out
on clear nights when the conditions are right
to lay on a blanket with those you love,
gazing at the heavens as light dances
rivers of color across the sky.

ORB WEAVER

You create round rugs of crystal light, masterpieces
drawn with silk straight from the sun, heaven-sent strands
drenched with awe, delicate brushstrokes on a work of art
dropped straight from a place of magic
–but look–
not all of us know how to weave orbs that shine
as if infused by wonder
...so will you show me how?
I imagine it's like tasting
a diamond's luster
or feeling a translucent beauty wash bare skin
or hearing angels slinging love straight into your marrow
–am I right?
Well, anyway, it's not your job to tell me,
so I'll imagine a world
where bones are lightning and skin's a mirror,
bark and soil, claw and fin portals to a realm
where everything alive, from
spiders to willows to polar bears to trout to moss to cats
along with any number of humans across the globe
weave webs of wonder from light that lingers
long after the world tries to snuff it out.

HOPE FOR THE WORLD

Can you ever have enough of this world?
…all its stillness and rainstorms
bright transitions and calls to move slower
reminders that moments passing
are reasons to savor
and no one has figured out yet
how to hoard that kind of pleasure
and I hope they never do.

−after Teddy Macker

THE LIVING MOUNTAIN

...catches lightning with hands
reaching toward the sky, no matter
how weathered those hands are,
speaks in snow melt creeks
making a path through
every sort of terrain
holds stories old
and stories just becoming
a pulse felt deep enough
to animate ancient earth
an invitation to live the questions
that allow all things to become possible
when trees are sentient and rocks whisper wonderments.

—*after Nan Shepherd*

CLOAKS OF LIGHT,
SCARVES OF SOUND

Dress for the job you want, they say.

So you sit still enough, long enough

to allow dawn's late winter fog

to seep deep into your pores, rolling

across the water to adorn you like a second skin.

You wait to move

until the sun crests the eastern tree line,

great orange orb of energy rising swiftly

to become a cloak of light.

Sandhill cranes and geese offer you scarves of sound

voices calling a greeting as wings beat overhead,

as the last of the lake ice melts

gifting you just enough acquiescence

to be here now, wearing the wild.

THE GREATEST NATURE POEM EVER

...starts with bold statements, declarations
of appreciative love for wildness of all sorts—
biting ants & jumping spiders
beach grass & bent twigs
shifting sand & falling raindrops,
(these declarations can be more subtle than bold, really, it can go either way)
anyone willing to acknowledge their place
in that wild family of things, and let's not forget
a robust description of wind dancing through ripples on still waters
or the way a full moon casts shadows of illumination on snow capped hills
along with enough left unsaid to keep imagination alive in wonder—
that love, however it presents itself, paves the way,
but not like a road through woods—
more like a trickle of water molding rock over eons, a steady presence
making itself known, persistent in its unrelenting reach, its unwavering way
of continuing to be, year
after year
after year,
reminding everything
that everything is a part
of nature's universal heart.
It keeps going after that, becoming more itself
every time you, and you, and you, too, take that love
(bold or not)
and make it your own—because you, too
are an essential part of the greatest nature poem ever.

−after Brian Doyle

HISTORY LESSONS

It's strange to look back
over your own work
and see the lessons a past version of yourself
has for who you are now.
You might see history repeating itself
for better or worse
or new possibilities
filtering in between the lines,
wisdom that found you then
reaching through time to lift you up now.

ATTUNEMENT

Look for the easy yes
sitting in plain sight
between the begrudging maybe
and the hard pass.
Find it like a ray of sunshine
finds a weed in the midst of rubble
or like a butterfly finds milkweed
in the middle of a city—
senses finely tuned
to that which fills you up
with the sustenance you need
in order to thrive.

SURVIVAL BY IMPERFECTION

What if you were a tree,
one who survived a clearcut
because you were deemed unfit
to become timber? If seeing flaws
can save a tree, just think
what accepting yours could do
if you let them be there, standing
tall in a field of felled perfection.

TEACHING THE WORLD TO SURVIVE

When your healing is imperfect
it's easy to beat yourself up
or knock yourself down
but beating yourself up
is a fight you can't win
and knocking yourself down
is a sure way to stay there.
Instead, take your imperfect healing
and hold it softly, cradled
like a delicate speckled egg—beautiful yet breakable,
powerful because of that vulnerability.
Hold it gently, offer a safe place,
a place it can live inside you
nestled as only imperfect things can nestle,
just there, against your heart, keeping time
with the pulse, life-force reminding you
healing isn't something you're graded on.
Healing is any wound, stitched and tended
becoming a scar equipped to share stories
intent on teaching the world to survive.

Church

/CHərCH/ *noun*

.

....wherever you find the version of God
that you know

CHURCH OF SHADOW & LIGHT

You know your holy places
by how accepting they are
of your whole personhood
by what you'll endure
to be there to pray
by the simple knowledge
that something shifts
each time you show up.

I go to the garden when I'm feeling unmoored, when I'm not sure
what to do next, or when I'm wondering when anything will ever
change for the better. Because even though every year I'm sure I won't
have the energy to plant the seeds or the time to tend the plants—or
weather and wildlife seem intent on destruction—the possibility of
something good growing, no matter what the conditions, keeps me
coming back year after year.

Something shifts each time I show up.

I go to the woods or the prairie, no matter how hot or cold the air
outside, to remember to be alive with my whole self; to join the
seemingly inaccessible wilds that live in each of us with something
deeper than what I can access on my own; to claim the pace that serves
my life best, one that allows a simple existence, one that is attuned
to the joys and sorrows of an earthly life; to ensure my quest for a
life worth living is underlaid with enough faith to keep me going for
another day.

Something shifts each time I show up.

WE ARE ONE BODY

Care for the world you live in
in all the ways available,
from how your feet touch the earth
to what nourishes and sustains you
to where you place your attention—
be sure your energy, your force of life,
goes toward only what is capable
of giving life, of accepting a full
spectrum of feeling, of adding to all
that is healing and essential
for true restoration.

IN AUGUST

The guy who sells sweet corn
from the back of an el camino
sets up shop with his wife
where the highway curves into town,
handpainted signs announcing
the start of summer's end
while heat ripples off the pavement
and afternoons stretch and laze
lingering even as time seems to slip
through my fingers like sand,
light slowly leaving to fill the moments
between the shifting sands
with shadow's holy presence.

UNNAMEABLE

It's been said that God is raindrops
on yellow leaves that have fallen to the ground,

beginnings and endings, even large stretches
of seemingly unremarkable time,

hot tea and the love that pours
when you make a cup for another

the way uncertainty waltzes
with deep knowing

how contrast contains
the beauty of light dancing with the dark.

Somehow all these details weave together
into a presence I, and maybe you, know as God.

TREATY

Sunlight and shadow
fall together toward illumination
and even hard days offer
a chance to grow
seedlings of
peace.

THE GOD I KNOW

The God I know
has lots of sons
and daughters
and those who don't
identify with either of those labels.

The God I know
walks the streets
and carries water;
sits with those who
know nothing but pain.

The God I know
is the bedrock of the land,
the crash of the ocean
and forgotten paths
up the back of the mountain.

The God I know
loves without borders
and seeps into parts
of the world that seem devoid of light,

carrying a whisper of something
we may never understand
in a language we knew
before we were born.

THE GOD I KNOW, PART TWO

The God I know
walks across borders,
children in hand,
because it's the only thing
left to do.

The God I know
rocks toddlers
who shiver in fear
because what they know
feels gone forever.

The God I know
walks with parents
who wonder what they could have done
while worry sits, silent and heavy
on their shoulders.

The God I know
whispers in the ears
of those who wonder about following orders
from others who are afraid
of what it means to love your neighbor.

The God I know
loves without limits
and weeps into the parts
of the world that seem far too broken—
that God wants us to remember

there is no such thing
as other people's children
and we belong to each other,
just like the source of all things
belongs to all, unwavering even today.

THE GOD I KNOW, PART THREE

The God I know
sits on the street with those
closest to fear as pain and grief collide.

The God I know
wonders when we will figure out
what it truly means to love one another.

The God I know
reminds us that thoughts
and prayers alone aren't enough.

The God I know
calls for right action, the sort that
opens hearts and minds in new ways.

The God I know
points to a bridge, one with
the capacity to carry heavy loads.

The God I know
walks across the bridge
to offer peace to a stranger.

The God I know
whispers continually that not
all is lost even when we think it is.

THE GOD I KNOW, PART FOUR

The God I know
is Rizpah on the mountain
seeking justice for her boys.

The God I know
sees color in a way that
honors stories of the other.

The God I know
calls us all into figuring out
what it means to be a good neighbor.

The God I know
isn't afraid to show up
in inconvenient places.

The God I know
remains, even amidst
uncertainty, confusion and heartache.

The God I know
is clear that while we may be one human race,
the color white has wielded power for too long.

The God I know
moves to crack and crumble privilege
into something that looks more like love.

THE GOD I KNOW, PART FIVE

The God I know
doesn't ban love from church
when some people don't agree
with how love presents itself.

The God I know
doesn't underwrite decisions
that claim some lifestyles
are more holy than others.

The God I know
doesn't strengthen rules
that exclude and shame
in the name of praise.

The God I know
doesn't inspire interpretations
of the Word that say, "you're wrong."
You love who you love, and that's beautiful.

The God I know
opens hearts
minds
doors
to unify all people
through every storm,
no matter who you love.

THE GOD I KNOW, PART SIX

The God I know
adds love to spaces between
everywhere across the globe.

The God I know
sits with kids who need school to feel safe/fed/heard,
parents and teachers doing the best they can with the tools they have.

The God I know
walks next to the unhoused,
those ordered to shelter in a place they didn't have.

The God I know
heals through the hands of many
offering peace when war seems to be waged from within.

The God I know
cradles the sick and those who love them
with a story that promises death isn't the end.

The God I know
fills a newly quiet earth
with birdsong and clear skies at dawn.

The God I know
is the truth of trauma and miracle
existing side by side.

THE GOD I KNOW, PART SEVEN

The God I know
is still on the mountain, Rizpah
seeking justice for her boys.

The God I know
is a Black man face down on pavement
gasping for breath at the hands of police.

The God I know
is more outraged by white supremacy's violence
than church doors ordered shut.

The God I know
is a white person
confronting her own racist ideals.

The God I know
is calling us all in
to do the anti-racist work

of rebuilding the kingdom
one truth at a time until
all lives really do matter.

THE GOD I KNOW
(DESPITE EVERYTHING)

The God I know
doesn't occupy lands
and support the oppression
of a people for decade
after decade.

The God I know
doesn't kill the children
of one people
to liberate the children
of another.

The God I know
doesn't condone violence
of any kind as justice
no matter how righteous
that violence seems to some.

The God I know
sits with parents of children lost and living
on both sides of the blockade
as they do their best to tend their pain
and embody love in a war zone.

The God I know
keeps laying bricks
on the bridge to peace
even when more parts of that bridge
are blasted away every day.

The God I know
helps bear loads too heavy
to carry up mountains
we may not summit
in this lifetime.

The God I know
takes the packs of the weary,
sets the table with hope, and
invites us to sit together to listen
long enough to find a new way forward.

EMBODIED CEASEFIRE

It may be
you feel at war
with a stranger.

It may be
you feel at war
with a neighbor.

It may be
you feel at war
with a friend.

It may be
you feel at war
with yourself.

Do you feel it—the war—when you find it inside?
How its violence wants to feed
on fear or uncertainty or pain?

Too much or not enough, be it space, food, or love
can make a battle feel like the only option
on the quest to live how you want to.

So if that, any of it,
even just a morsel,
tastes true for you...

feel the war—
(usually best done with the support
of someone you trust)

where it wants to live in your body
how it yearns to break out
what it wants to destroy—

and allow the war, whatever wants a fight
—whatever pulses with need to prove power-over—
allow it a chance to float to the surface (don't force it),

where it can rest
on the calm waters of your skin
as you breathe

or rush alongside
tumbling cascades
as you sweat it out.

It won't be comfortable.
But it's on its way
to becoming something else

something seen, felt, and heard; acknowledged
long enough to allow a letting go, claws softening
into that which may, in time, allow an embodied peace.

SMALL THINGS AT THE END OF A YEAR THAT'S TOO MUCH

Offer me a ticket to the rain
and I'll meet you there
where water drops in curtains
that pool at our feet
while we walk hand in hand
through what can't be bought
to find what can't be sold.

—on peace as the only way forward

DIRT CHURCH

Is where I pray, a place
to witness light spilling into a new day
even when the blood shed yesterday
is not yet dry.

Is where I pray, a place
to absorb warm sun on my face
when the rest of me
feels numb with grief.

Is where I pray, a place
to notice a butterfly's delicate beauty
keeping company with overripe fruit
entering a season of decay.

Is where I pray, a place
to be wholly alive
on this hurting earth,
each day a new union of sunlight and shadow.

THESE QUESTIONS SOUND RIDICULOUS, BUT THE ANSWERS ARE ANYONE'S GUESS

Rumi said *"The war is over. The band is singing. Come and dance."*

What if the war was really over? Would the world know what to do? Would you know what to do? Would I? Would anybody? How would we cope with peace? Would it leave us feeling anxious or unmoored or without a way to pursue purpose? What brings people together more than conflict or the quest to garner enough power to create change? Maybe we'd feel adrift, wondering where to put our energy, the energy we used to put toward praying for and working toward peace. What happens when you get what you want?

Would we be able to go, and dance?

UNIVERSAL PEACE NOW

Whatever the state of things
what role can you play
that brings peace?

Say what you will about war (outside yourself and within)–
where are the cracks in fighting
that illuminate other ways?

Find the calm blue flame
in a sea of fiery red.

–after Rumi

TAKE MY HAND AND COME ALONG

It is no small thing
to do something, together
when you could do nothing, alone.

CARTOGRAPHIES OF PEACE

A while later, all at once the birds lift as one, a giant murmuration of sound soaring over still waters into the horizon beyond, silence stretching out in their absence, leaving a longing for a world where people are like birds, a new kind of murmuration coalescing only for peace, within and expanding over all, guns laid down between shadows and light, coating the land with goodness and grace, creating new soft places to land.

The road is winding, and I take it anyway. Winding roads give texture enough to enhance the hours.

Listen to the war within yourself—what does it have to say about what it means to be peace?

Sunbursts always find a way to bleed light through darkness.

May we all find those soft places to land, whether the search keeps us tending home fires or journeying deep into the dark and shadowy places that aren't on the map. May we create cartographies that allow space for all that gives life. May we be the mapmakers who outline a world where peace reigns.

Every moment is the end of something and the beginning of something else. What ends now? And what begins?

ACKNOWLEDGMENTS

Infinite gratitude to everyone who has walked beside me during my own seasons of shadow, who has brought light enough to see a new path, and who has been part of the community I've come to know as church. No book comes into being without the support of many, so if you've supported me, thank you. It means more than I can say.

Extra thanks are due to Nick and Eva Barr, Mom, Dad, Connor Wolfe, Holly Walsh, Becca Long, and Becs Zelis. Thank you for believing in me during a time when it was easy to not believe in myself.

NOTES

The title poem, "Church of Shadow & Light" was first published in my 2023 book *Collisions of Earth and Sky* (published by Broadleaf Books, an imprint of 1517 Media).

Several of the poems in "The God I Know" series were previously published in *Cold Spring Hallelujah* and *Slouching Toward Radiance*. "Unnameable" also first appeared in *Cold Spring Hallelujah* in a slightly different form.

The bulk of these poems came into being thanks to a year-long writing course called *Writing the Wild* (lead by Krissy Kludt and J. Drew Lanham) which I participated in from September 2023 to June 2024. During that time was one of the warmest Minnesota winters I've ever experienced. I was also laid off from my full time coaching job in January 2024, an experience I've had before, but one that always has quite a bit of influence over any writing that emerges during the uncertain days that follow such a life event.

"Instructions for Living" was first published in Birchbark Editing's *MicroLit Almanac* in August 2024.

The poem "Dirt Church" is a slightly reworked version of "A Complicated Joy" which was first published in *Slouching Toward Radiance* (Wayfarer Books, 2022). The alternative title is inspired by a line in "Sassafras", a song by Rising Appalachia.

ABOUT THE AUTHOR

Heidi Barr is a writer and wellness coach whose work is founded on a commitment to cultivating ways of being that are life-giving and sustainable for people, communities, and the planet. She is the author of several books of creative nonfiction, including *Collisions of Earth and Sky* and *Woodland Manitou*, and co author of *12 Tiny things*. She's also authored two other poetry collections, one cookbook, and is editor of "The Mindful Kitchen," a wellness column in *The Wayfarer Magazine*. One of the inaugural Poets of Place for the lower St. Croix Valley, her poetry has been featured in numerous publications, including the *St. Paul Almanac* and *South Dakota in Poems*. She lives with her family in rural Minnesota, where they tend a large vegetable garden, explore nature, and do their best to live simply.

Learn more at heidibarr.com.

At Wayfarer Books we believe poetry is the language of the earth. We believe words—shaped like rivers through wild places—can change the shape of the world. We publish poets and writers and renegades who stand outside of mainstream culture—poets, essayists, and storytellers whose work might withstand the scrutiny of crows and coyotes, those who are cryptic and floral, the crepuscular, and the queer-at-heart. We are more than just a publisher but a community of writers. Our mission is to produce books that can serve as a compass and map to all wayfarers through wild terrain.

wayfarerbooks.org